Henry VIII

by Harriet Castor
Illustrations by Peter Kent

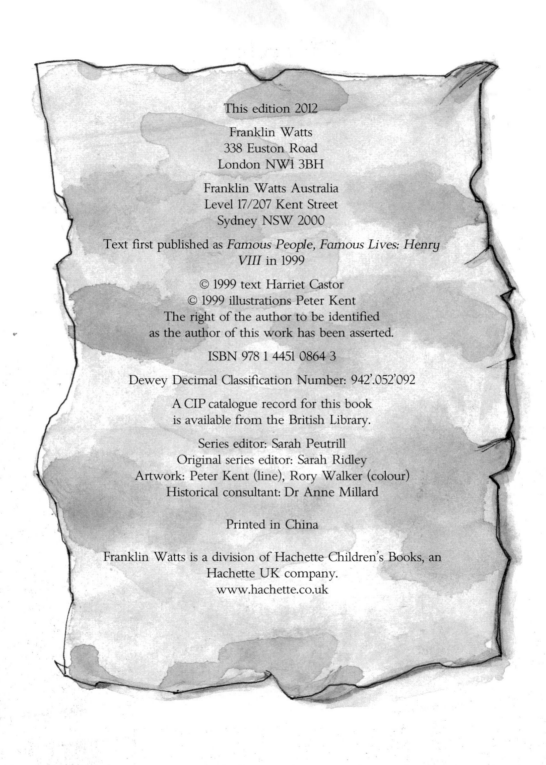

This edition 2012

Franklin Watts
338 Euston Road
London NW1 3BH

Franklin Watts Australia
Level 17/207 Kent Street
Sydney NSW 2000

Text first published as *Famous People, Famous Lives: Henry VIII* in 1999

ISBN 978 1 4451 0864 3

Dewey Decimal Classification Number: 942'.052'092

A CIP catalogue record for this book
is available from the British Library.

Series editor: Sarah Peutrill
Original series editor: Sarah Ridley
Artwork: Peter Kent (line), Rory Walker (colour)
Historical consultant: Dr Anne Millard

Printed in China

Franklin Watts is a division of Hachette Children's Books, an
Hachette UK company.
www.hachette.co.uk

Chapter 1

In 1501 there was a royal wedding in London.
The King and Queen's eldest son, Prince
Arthur, married a Spanish princess called
Catherine of Aragon. Arthur's younger brother,
Henry, led Catherine up the aisle.

Henry had grown up thinking he was going to be an important nobleman, or perhaps a powerful priest.

But five months after the wedding, Prince Arthur fell ill and died. Now Henry was the heir to the throne. His father made sure he was kept safe.

Then, when Henry was seventeen, his father died too. Henry became King Henry VIII.

One of the first things Henry did as king was to marry Catherine, the Spanish princess who was his brother's widow.

Royal marriages were a good way of making an alliance, or friendship, between countries. Spain was an important country. Besides, Henry and Catherine liked each other.

Because Catherine was the widow of Henry's brother, Henry had to ask the Pope for special permission to marry her. The Pope said yes.

Chapter 2

Henry was everyone's idea of what a king should be. He was tall, handsome and sporty. He was good at languages and music. He loved hunting, dancing, feasting and wearing fine clothes.

Government meetings bored Henry, and he hated writing letters. But he made sure his ministers told him everything that happened. They left all the most important decisions to him.

Henry's chief minister was a priest called Cardinal Wolsey. Unlike most people at Court, Wolsey hadn't been born into an important family.

Wolsey was clever and worked hard, and Henry trusted him. Many of the nobles were jealous of Wolsey's power. They especially hated him because he came from an ordinary family.

Wolsey's palace is magnificent.

Henry believed great kings should be great warriors, so he wanted to go to war. He decided to attack France, one of England's oldest enemies.

Henry sailed to France with his army. He didn't take part in the fighting himself, but his soldiers won a battle. Henry came home triumphant.

Soon the old French king died. The new king, François I, was young and athletic. Henry was curious to meet him, so Wolsey arranged it.

The meeting took place on the border between Calais – a town England owned then – and the rest of France. Everywhere was decorated with gold cloth, so people called the place 'The Field of the Cloth-of-Gold'.

Chapter 3

Henry and Catherine had been married for nearly twenty years. They had had several children, but only one had survived: a daughter, Mary.

A woman can't rule! It would be a disaster!

Henry wanted a son. He thought that only men were good at ruling countries.

Then Henry fell in love with one of Catherine's maids of honour, Anne Boleyn. She was young, witty and clever. He wanted to marry her.

I'm sure Anne could give me a son.

It is God's punishment that we have no sons!

Henry had begun to think that God was cross with him for marrying Catherine, his brother's widow.

He wanted the new Pope to say that, in God's eyes, they had never truly been married. The trouble was, Catherine's nephew Charles was the King of Spain. He was very powerful. The Pope knew that if he agreed to do what Henry wanted, Charles would be angry.

The Pope made promises to both Charles and Henry. But he didn't keep them. Eventually, he sent a cardinal (an important priest) to England to judge the case for divorce. The cardinal he chose was old and ill.

When the case began, Catherine knelt at Henry's feet. She said she was his true wife. Then she left the courtroom and refused to come back.

Still there was no decision. Henry was angry. He blamed Wolsey and sent him to prison. But Wolsey fell ill and died on the way.

Then Anne Boleyn became pregnant. Henry had to marry her quickly so that the baby could be next-in-line to the throne.

So Henry's ministers persuaded Parliament to pass a law saying that Henry was head of the Church in England, and he could judge the divorce case himself. Henry divorced Catherine.

Chapter 4

At this time, people all over Europe were arguing about the right way to worship God. One group, Catholics, supported the Pope. Another group, later called Protestants, were against the Pope. Many people were put to death.

Henry didn't like either side. He was against the Pope, but he was also against many things the Protestants believed in.

Henry wanted his subjects to believe only what he told them.

Henry ordered that every monastery and nunnery should be shut down. His new chief minister, Thomas Cromwell, organised it for him.

Henry said it was because the monks and nuns weren't living a holy life. They were greedy and lazy. This was true in some cases but not all. Many of the monasteries had lots of money and land, which Henry wanted.

Chapter 5

Meanwhile, Anne had her baby. It was a girl, called Elizabeth. Henry was disappointed and cancelled his planned celebrations. He didn't know that Elizabeth would one day be a great ruler.

Still no son! God must think this marriage is wrong, too.

What's her name?

Jane Seymour, Your Grace.

Anne got pregnant twice more, but lost the babies. Henry was angry. He had already fallen in love with someone else: one of Anne's ladies-in-waiting, called Jane Seymour.

Anne was put in prison. She was accused of plotting to murder Henry and of having affairs with several men. None of it was true, but Anne and the men had their heads chopped off. Straight afterwards, Henry married Jane.

The next year Jane had a baby boy, Edward. But Jane died a few days later. Henry was very sad.

Because royal marriages were a useful way of making friendships between countries, Thomas Cromwell started looking for a new wife for Henry right away.

Whenever a possible wife was suggested, Henry wanted to know what she looked like. So the famous painter, Hans Holbein, was sent to paint her.

One of the people Holbein painted was the daughter of a German duke – Anne of Cleves.

Henry agreed to marry Anne. When she landed in England, he was so impatient to meet her that he arrived early, in disguise.

But Henry didn't like what he saw. He was angry with Cromwell for arranging the marriage.

Many of the nobles were glad. They were jealous of Cromwell's power and hated him because, like Wolsey, he came from an ordinary family.

Henry had already noticed a new young woman at Court. Her name was Katherine Howard.

The Howards were powerful nobles who hated Cromwell. They began plotting against him.

Cromwell was put in the Tower of London. As Henry's minister, he had invented a new way for important prisoners to be executed without trial. It was used for the first time – on him.

Cromwell worked hard for Henry. Henry will regret this ...

Another wife! How many will he have?

Since Henry was Head of the Church, it was easy for him to divorce Anne of Cleves. Anne didn't argue. Henry gave her plenty of money to live on.

Now Henry was free to marry his sweetheart, Katherine Howard.

Chapter 6

Katherine was five years younger than Mary, Henry's daughter. She was cheerful and lively, but foolish, too. Before her marriage, Katherine had had several secret lovers.

She had fallen in love with an ambitious but charming courtier called Thomas Culpeper. Soon she started seeing him again.

Bring me a sword! I'll kill her myself.

Like every powerful family, the Howards had enemies. Some of them found out about Katherine's affair and told Henry. Henry was grief-stricken and furious. He had Katherine and her lover executed.

As his sixth wife Henry chose a young widow called Catherine Parr. She was intelligent, and kind to his children. She was also good at nursing Henry.

At last, aged fifty-five, Henry died. He was buried, as he'd ordered, next to Jane Seymour at Windsor Castle.

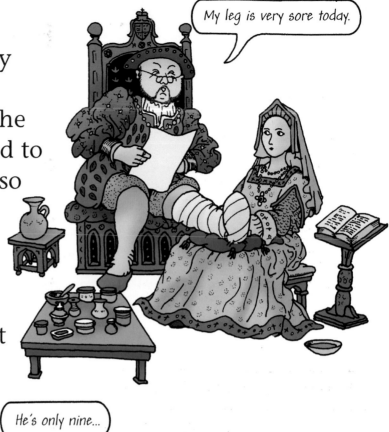

My leg is very sore today.

Long live King Edward!

He's only nine...

Their son – the boy Henry had longed for – became King Edward VI.

29

Further facts

Rhyme to remember

There is a rhyme that makes it easy to remember what happened to each of Henry's six wives:

 Divorced, beheaded, died,
 Divorced, beheaded, survived.

Can you name them all?

H&A, H&K, H&C, H&J

In Henry's time, royal buildings were often decorated with the royal initials. Sometimes the old initials survive. Today, if you go to St James's Palace in London, for example, you can still see the initials of Henry and Anne Boleyn.

Tudor family

Henry's family name was Tudor. His father, Henry VII, was the first Tudor king. Henry VIII hoped that the Tudor family would reign for a long time. In fact, they lasted only as long as his children. All three became monarchs – but none of them had children, so the Tudor line came to an end.

Some important dates in Henry VIII's lifetime

1491 Henry is born in Greenwich, near London, the third child of King Henry VII and his wife, Elizabeth of York.

1502 Arthur, Prince of Wales – Henry's older brother – dies.

1509 Henry VII dies and Henry becomes King Henry VIII.

1509 Henry marries his brother's widow, Catherine of Aragon.

1516 Henry and Catherine's daughter, Princess Mary, is born.

1520 Henry meets the young French King, François I, at the Field of the Cloth-of-Gold.

1533 Henry declares that the Pope has no special authority in England; he is now Head of the Church of England.

1533 Queen Anne Boleyn gives birth to a girl, Princess Elizabeth.

1537 Queen Jane Seymour gives birth to a boy, Prince Edward. Jane dies twelve days later.

1540 Henry marries Anne of Cleves. They divorce soon after.

1540 Henry marries Katherine Howard.

1543 Henry marries Catherine Parr.

1547 Henry dies, aged fifty-five. He is buried in St George's Chapel, Windsor Castle.

Quiz

Can you remember?

1. Who had Henry VIII's first wife been married to before him?

2. What country did Henry go to war against?

3. When Henry went to meet the new French king what was their meeting place called?

4. From whom did Henry have to ask permission for a divorce from Catherine of Aragon?

5. What were Henry's wives called?

6. What happened to each of his wives?

7. What were Henry's children called?

8. What did Henry want more than anything else and why?

Answers on page 32

Glossary

Court The name for the wealthy and important people in the country, and their servants, who regularly visited the king in whichever palace he was living.

Courtroom The place or room in which a court of law meets.

Government The group of people who help to run the country and decide what laws will be made.

Heir The person who will be given the property or title of someone else after their death.

Lady-in-waiting/ Maid of Honour A young woman from a wealthy background who acts as a helper and friend to the Queen. Unmarried ladies-in-waiting were called maids of honour.

Ministers The most powerful people in the government.

Nobles The wealthiest and most powerful landowners.

Pope The head of the Catholic Church.

Index

Quiz answers

1. His brother, Arthur
2. France
3. The Field of the Cloth-of-Gold
4. The Pope
5. Catherine of Aragon, Anne Boleyn, Jane Seymour, Anne of Cleves, Katherine Howard, Catherine Parr
6. Divorced, beheaded, died, divorced, beheaded, survived
7. Mary, Elizabeth, Edward
8. A son – to be King when Henry died